70 THOUSAND, MILLION, MILLION, MILLION STARS IN SPACE

PAUL ROCKETT

FRANKLIN WATTS

LONDON • SYDNEY

First published in 2014 by Franklin Watts

Franklin Watts
338 Euston Road
London NW1 3BH

Franklin Watts Australia
Level 17/207 Kent Street
Sydney, NSW 2000

Editor: Rachel Cooke
Design and illustration: Mark Ruffle
www.rufflebrothers.com

Dewey number: 520
HB ISBN: 978 1 4451 2671 5
Library ebook ISBN: 978 1 4451 2677 7

Printed in China

Franklin Watts is a division of Hachette
Children's Books, an Hachette UK company.
www.hachette.co.uk

Picture credits: Art Archive/Alamy: 22t; Marcel Clemens/Shutterstock: 11t; ESA/Hubble/NASA: 9tr; Peter Horree/Alamy: 21tr; Hubble data: NASA, ESA and A.Zeus ; GALEX data: NASA, JPL-CALech, GALEX Team, J.Huchra et al ; Spitzer data: NASA/ JPL/CAltech/S. Willner. All Harvard-Smithsonian Center for Astrophysics: 9tl; Iryna1/Shutterstock: 21cl; Panos Karas/Shutterstock: 20tr; NASA/JPL/ Caltech: 9tc; NASA/JPL/Space Science Institute: 16tr; Nicku/Shutterstock: 20bl, 20br, 21cr; Charles O'Rear/ Corbis: 7bl; Vadim Petrakov/Shuttterstock: 23bl; Photo Researchers/Alamy: 21br; Subaru/NASA/JPL-Caltech: 4tl.

Throughout the book you are given data relating to various pieces of information covering the topic. The numbers will most likely be an estimation based on research made over a period of time and in a particular area. Some other research may reach a different set of data, and all these figures may change with time as new research and information is gathered. The numbers provided within this book are believed to be correct at the time of printing and have been sourced from the following sites: astro.cornell.edu; astrosociety.org; astronomy. com; bbc.co.uk; bluebookarchive.org; burro.cwru. edu; cometography.com; computerweekly.com; cosmotography.com; curious.astro.cornell.edu; dailygalaxy.com; deepsky.org.uk; earth-central.weebly. com; edition.cnn.com; electronics.howstuffworks. com; esa.int; extremetech.com; factsforkids.net; forteantimes.com; geography.about.com; heasarc. nasa.gov; hours.geocosmic.org; howitworksdaily. com; iau.org; iop.org; kidsastronomy.com; lasp. colorado.edu; messenger-education.org; mnn.com; murderousmaths.co.uk; nasa.gov; news.discovery. com; news.nationalgeographic.com; npr.org; pbs. org; physicsoftheuniverse.com; ras.org.uk; rense. com; reuters.com; science.nationalgeographic. com; sciencedaily.com; solarsystem.nasa.gov; space. com; spacefellowship.com; starchild.gsfc.nasa.gov; ufoevidence.org; universetoday.com; worldufoday.com.

CONTENTS

The Universe contains everything that we know and more. It is a size which is so big, it is difficult for us to imagine. However, many astronomers believe that about **14,000,000,000 years ago** the Universe was thousands of times smaller than a pinhead. Then, this tiny dot suddenly exploded, an event called the Big Bang. From this explosion grew the Universe and it is still expanding in size today.

WHAT WE CAN OBSERVE

When talking about the Universe and all the galaxies, planets and stars inside it, astronomers are mostly talking about the 'observable universe'. This consists of everything that can be detected by modern technology. We may be unable to see or count any objects beyond the observable universe, but we know that the following exists within it:

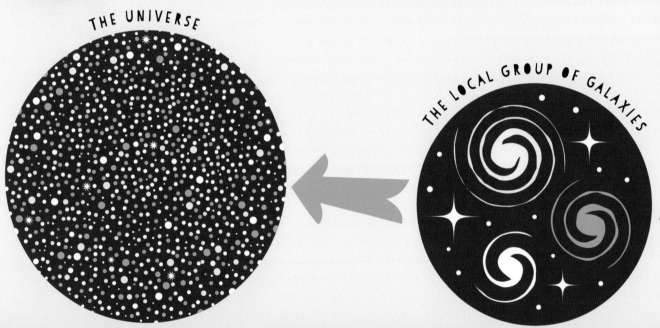

THE UNIVERSE

THE LOCAL GROUP OF GALAXIES

MEASURING THE UNIVERSE

Astronomers use light travel to measure how far away things are in space. Light is incredibly fast – it can travel about seven times around the Earth in one second!

One light-year = 9,461,000,000,000 km
One light-month = 777,060,000,000 km
One light-week = 181,300,000,000 km
One light-day = 25,900,000,000 km
One light-hour = 1,008,000,000 km
One light-minute = 17,098,000 km
One light-second = 299,792 km

VIEWING THE UNIVERSE

The pollution from large cities and industrialisation make it difficult for us to get a clear view of the stars and planets in the night sky.
This was not such a problem for astronomers in the past, who began mapping the Universe from what they could see with the naked eye.

In the 1600s, the invention of the telescope meant that astronomers could see three to four times further into space.

Today, astronomers view the Universe through large observatories and study computer data collected from satellites and space missions out in the Solar System.

HYDRA

CRUX

CONSTELLATIONS

Some of the stars in the night sky are grouped into constellations. There are **88 constellations**. They are formations of stars that join up like a dot-to-dot puzzle to look like a creature or an object.

Constellations are often used as a way of mapping the sky, helping sailors to navigate at night. The largest constellation is Hydra; it is made up of **16 main stars** and is said to represent a water snake. The smallest constellation is the Crux or Southern Cross. This is made up of **four stars**.

THE MILKY WAY

OUR SOLAR SYSTEM

EARTH

Measurements of light travel are categorised into periods of time:
one light-year is the measurement of how fast light can travel within one year.

(nine trillion, four hundred and sixty-one billion)
(seven hundred and seventy-seven billion and sixty million)
(one hundred and eighty-one billion, three hundred million)
(twenty-five billion, nine hundred million)
(one billion, eight hundred)
(seventeen million and ninety-eight million)
(two hundred and ninety-nine thousand, seven hundred and ninety-two)

A scientist once said that: 'The total number of stars in the Universe is larger than all the grains of sand on all the beaches of the planet Earth.'

The number of stars in space and the number of grains of sand on Earth can only be estimated. An advanced telescope can count the stars within a small area of our galaxy. This number can then be multiplied by the size of our galaxy which can then be multiplied by the number of galaxies within the Universe, providing an estimate to the number of stars in space.

THERE ARE 70 THOUSAND, MILLION, MILLION, MILLION STARS IN THE UNIVERSE.

This number can also be written as 70 sextillion and when written in numerals it looks like this: •••••••••••••

70,000,000,000,000,000,000,000

THERE ARE SEVEN THOUSAND FIVE HUNDRED MILLION, MILLION, MILLION GRAINS OF SAND ON THE PLANET EARTH.

This number can also be written as seven quintillion, five hundred quadrillion and when written in numerals it looks like this: •••••••••••••

7,500,000,000,000,000,000

ESTIMATES

Estimates are not exact amounts, but are educated guesses based on the best information available. Not all galaxies are the same and so the final number of stars is unlikely to be correct.

WHAT IS A STAR?

A star is a ball of hot glowing gas. Inside a star are different gases that create a nuclear fusion which releases heat and light – this is why they shine.

A star is made up of approximately:

70% hydrogen ————————
28% helium ————————
1.4% carbon, nitrogen and oxygen —
0.5% other elements such as neon, iron, silicon, magnesium and sulphur. —

Apart from the Sun, the closest star to Earth is **Proxima Centauri**, which is **40,000,000,000,000 km** away.

The **Sun** is a star at the centre of our Solar System. Its distance from Earth depends on the position of Earth during Earth's orbit of the Sun, but on average it is **149,600,000 km** away.

Venus is the nearest planet to Earth; its distance varies depending on the orbit of both planets. Venus can be as close as **38,000,000 km** or as far as **261,000,000 km**. At its nearest point Venus can be seen in the night sky. It reflects light from the Sun and can look like an extremely bright star.

We can see the **Moon** in the night sky because it reflects light from the Sun. The average distance between the Earth and the Moon is **384,403 km**.

A **comet** is not a star, it is formed by bits of space dust and gas that collect into an icy form. They take their name from the Greek *aster kometes*, which means 'long-haired stars'. Comets are known to have come as close to the Earth as **50,000,000 km**.

Asteroids are not stars. They are bits of rock that have not managed to come together as large planets. In 2013, an asteroid came within **27,680 km** of Earth.

A **meteor** is a piece of space rock that enters the Earth's atmosphere. As it falls it begins to burn and becomes a fireball. Fiery falling meteors can look like fireworks which has led them to be called 'shooting stars' even though they are not stars.

Usually a meteor burns out into nothing as it heads towards the Earth, but sometimes meteors do collide with the Earth. A meteor that hits the Earth is called a meteorite.

This crater, in the Arizona Desert, USA, was caused by a meteorite.

THERE ARE 500 BILLION
GALAXIES IN THE UNIVERSE

The largest structures in the Universe are galaxy superclusters. These contain millions of galaxies and can measure hundreds of millions of light-years across.

Smaller groups of galaxies are called clusters.

Galaxies are collections of stars that are drawn to a common centre of gravity. Some are small with only a few million stars, while others could have as many as **400,000,000,000 stars** or more. Some scientists estimate that there are around **500,000,000,000 galaxies** in the Universe.

Most galaxies are gathered together in small clusters. Our galaxy, the Milky Way, is part of a cluster of galaxies called the Local Group.

There are about **30 galaxies** within the Local Group. The three largest are:

ANDROMEDA
2,500,000 light-years from Earth

MILKY WAY
Our galaxy

TRIANGULUM
3,000,000 light-years from Earth

HOW MANY STARS IN EACH GALAXY?

	TRILLIONS	BILLIONS	MILLIONS	THOUSANDS
ANDROMEDA	1 ⭐⭐⭐⭐⭐⭐⭐⭐⭐⭐⭐			
MILKY WAY	3 ⭐⭐⭐⭐⭐⭐⭐⭐⭐			
TRIANGULUM	4 ⭐⭐⭐⭐⭐⭐⭐⭐			

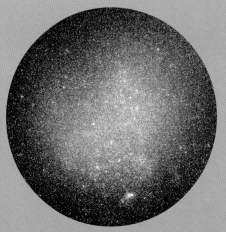

SPIRAL

Spiral galaxies have long arms that come out from the centre. New stars are created in the arms, with large stars causing the dust clouds around them to glow brightly. The three largest galaxies in the Local Group are spiral.

ELLIPTICAL

The stars within an elliptical galaxy are often very close together which can make the centre look like one giant star. New stars are not created in this galaxy. The stars it contains were created a very long time ago.

IRREGULAR

Any galaxy that doesn't look like a spiral or elliptical galaxy is categorised as an irregular galaxy.

MOVEMENT

All galaxies move through space.

They rotate around their centre with the speed of movement becoming slower as the galaxy material extends and spreads outwards.

A cluster of galaxies also rotates around a central point of gravity within that cluster.

GRAVITY

All the stars in a galaxy are kept together by the gravity of other stars and the gravity that is at the centre of each galaxy and cluster of galaxies.

Gravity is a force that attracts one object to another object. The movement of galaxies, planets and moons in space is due to their interaction with the gravitational pull from other objects. It is this force that holds the galaxies together, and the force that keeps planets and moons in their orbits.

THE MILKY WAY IS
13.2 BILLION YEARS OLD

The Milky Way is the galaxy that contains our solar system.

Some scientists believe the Milky Way to be as old as the Universe itself, whereas our solar system and planet Earth are much younger.

The Milky Way became its current size by eating other galaxies.

5%

Less than **5%** of the stars in the Milky Way are brighter or bigger than the Sun.

Billions of years old

14 13 12 11 10 9 8 7 6 5 4 3 2 1 0

MILKY WAY

EARTH

At the centre of the Milky Way is a giant black hole. It is estimated to be **27,000 light-years** from Earth and is four times bigger than the Sun. A black hole has an extremely powerful force of gravity which pulls everything towards it. Even light gets sucked in.

27,000 LIGHT-YEARS

WHERE DID THE MILKY WAY COME FROM?

There are uncertainties around how the Milky Way was formed. A lot of scientists think that during the Big Bang collections of gas and dust came together forming clusters that became galaxies.

As we are inside the galaxy we do not see it from Earth as a spiral, but as a thin band arching across the night sky. It appears as a pale, white glow, a sight that has led to the creation of many myths around its origin.

IN ROMAN, GREEK AND EGYPTIAN MYTHOLOGY, the Milky Way is believed to have formed from the spillage of milk.

THE KHOISAN PEOPLE from southern Africa believe that a young girl who wanted to visit people at night threw up embers from a fire into the sky so as to light her journey. This created the Milky Way.

IN ARMENIAN MYTHOLOGY, the Milky Way is called the 'Straw Thief's Way'. The god Vahagn stole some straw and fled across the heavens dropping bits along the way which created the Milky Way.

AN ANCIENT HINDU story sees all of the stars and planets above the Earth as moving through space like a dolphin. The Milky Way forms the stomach of the dolphin.

1,000,000,000,000,000,000 km wide

OUR SOLAR SYSTEM IS 11 BILLION KM WIDE

	QUINTILLION	QUADRILLION	TRILLION	BILLION	MILLION	THOUSAND
The Milky Way is about	1 0000	0000	0000	0000	000	KM WIDE
Our solar system is			11	0000	000	KM WIDE
The Earth is					12756	KM WIDE

In our solar system there are eight planets orbiting around the Sun.

MERCURY····· ● ·············· 58,000,000 km, 3.22 light-minutes from the Sun

VENUS······ ········· 108,000,000 km, 6.01 light-minutes

EARTH······· ········· 150,000,000 km, 8.32 light-minutes

MARS······ ········· 228,000,000 km, 12.7 light-minutes

JUPITER···· ········· 778,000,000 km, 43.3 light-minutes

SATURN·····

URANUS·····

NEPTUNE··

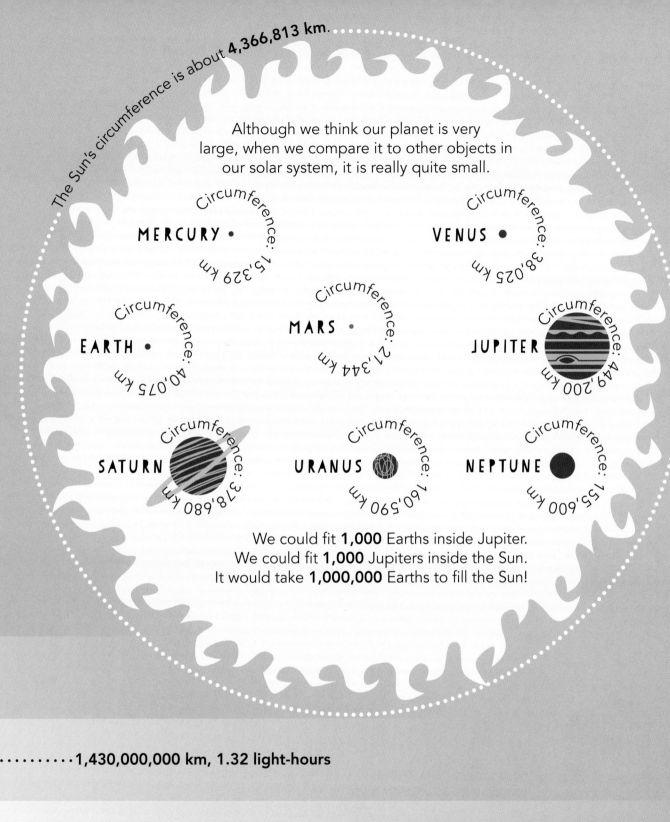

The Sun's circumference is about **4,366,813 km**.

Although we think our planet is very large, when we compare it to other objects in our solar system, it is really quite small.

MERCURY •
Circumference: 15,329 km

VENUS •
Circumference: 38,025 km

EARTH •
Circumference: 40,075 km

MARS •
Circumference: 21,344 km

JUPITER
Circumference: 449,200 km

SATURN
Circumference: 378,680 km

URANUS
Circumference: 160,590 km

NEPTUNE
Circumference: 155,600 km

We could fit **1,000** Earths inside Jupiter.
We could fit **1,000** Jupiters inside the Sun.
It would take **1,000,000** Earths to fill the Sun!

•••••••••••1,430,000,000 km, 1.32 light-hours

•••••••••••••2,880,000,000 km, 2.66 light-hours

•••••••••••••••••4,500,000,000 km, 4.16 light-hours •••••••••

Explorations into space have enabled scientists to learn a lot about the Earth's environment and have put satellites into space that allow us to communicate across the world with computers and phones. Astronauts have also gone into space to explore the possibility of humans living on the Moon and on other planets, as well as in space stations.

MISSIONS TO THE MOON

There have been **45 missions** to the Moon. Of these, only **19** landed successfully. The remaining **26** were either planned crash landings or didn't quite make it in one piece.

Only **six** of the missions to the Moon were manned.

US: 25

USSR: 14

INDIA: 1

CHINA: 1

EUROPEAN SPACE AGENCY: 1

JAPAN: 3

On 20 July 1969 the spacecraft Apollo 11 landed on the Moon. This was the first manned mission to the Moon and was broadcast live on television.

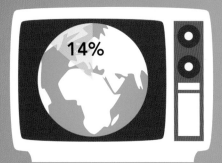

14%

An estimated **500,000,000 people** worldwide watched this event. That's around **14% of the total population** of the world at that time.

64GB OF MEMORY

= 1,048,576 X

APOLLO 11 COMPUTER POWER

The Apollo Guidance Computer (AGC), that was used to control Apollo 11, had approximately **64 KB** of memory. The average mobile phone today has far more computing power.

WHERE DID THEY LAND?

Apollo 16
Landed here:
27 April 1972

Apollo 17
Landed here:
11 December
1972

Apollo 12
Landed here:
24 November
1969

Apollo 15
Landed here:
7 August
1971

Apollo 14
Landed here:
5 February
1971

Apollo 11
Landed here:
20 July 1969

12
Number of people to have walked on the Moon.

530
Number of people to have gone into space.

No animal has been on the Moon but many different creatures have been sent into space. These include: monkeys, pigs, dogs, cats, guinea pigs, mice, rats, frogs, jellyfish, tortoises, snails and fruit flies.

ARE ALIENS LIVING 57 MILLION KM AWAY OR NEXT DOOR?

There is as yet no scientific evidence shown to prove the existence of aliens. However, there are some scientists who believe that aliens may live **57,000,000 km** away on Enceladus, one of Saturn's moons.

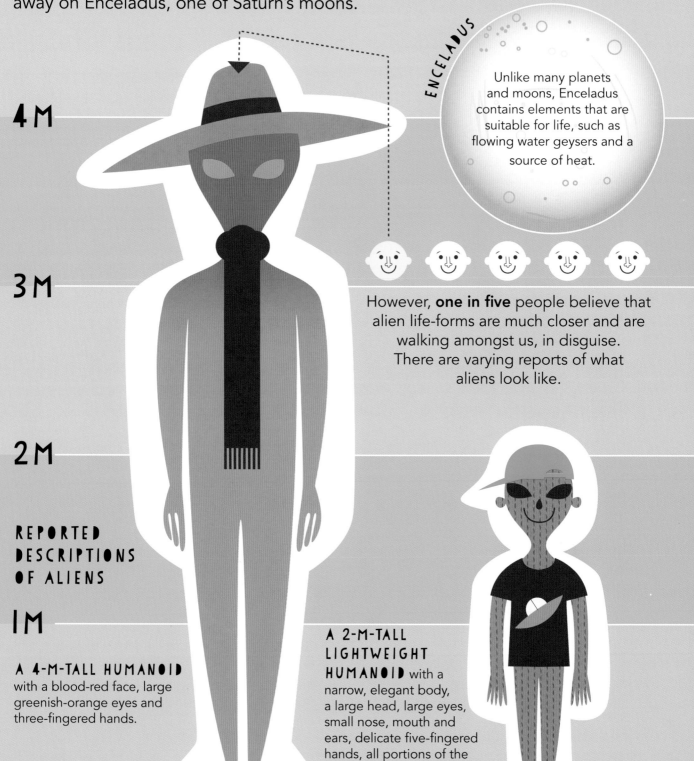

ENCELADUS

Unlike many planets and moons, Enceladus contains elements that are suitable for life, such as flowing water geysers and a source of heat.

However, **one in five** people believe that alien life-forms are much closer and are walking amongst us, in disguise. There are varying reports of what aliens look like.

4 M

3 M

2 M

REPORTED DESCRIPTIONS OF ALIENS

1 M

A 4-M-TALL HUMANOID with a blood-red face, large greenish-orange eyes and three-fingered hands.

A 2-M-TALL LIGHTWEIGHT HUMANOID with a narrow, elegant body, a large head, large eyes, small nose, mouth and ears, delicate five-fingered hands, all portions of the head and body covered with a soft, downy, neat fur.

UFOS

UFOs (unidentified flying objects) are believed to be alien vehicles from outer space. What a lot of people think of as UFOs usually turn out to be lights from vehicles, birds or odd-shaped clouds. However, a study into UFO sightings in the USA, between 1951 and 1954, found that out of 3,201 sightings 704 remained unidentified . . .

Results of investigations into UFO sightings:

1.0% birds

2% psychological

0.4% clouds

2.2% light phenomena

22% unknown origin (UFOs)

5% other

9% insufficient information

15% balloons

22% astronomical (stars and planets)

22% aircraft

A 1.5-M-TALL HUMANOID with a large bald head, small, sunken eyes, small concave nose with two nostrils, thin lipless mouth devoid of teeth and an ear hole on each side of the head with a tiny lobe. The longest part of the arm is between the elbow and the wrist and the hand has four long slender fingers with a suction pad on the end of each one.

THE MOST POPULAR DESCRIPTIONS FOR UFOS ARE:

1. Lights
2. Triangles
3. Circles

A 90-CM-TALL HUMANOID with a large hairless, earthy-green skinned head, large yellow-green hemispherical, protruding eyes with vertical pupils, no eyebrows or eye lashes and ring-like yellow-green eyelids at the base of the eye. The face has a large, long, straight nose. The mouth is a slit, shaped like a circumflex accent and continually opens and closes like a fish. The hands each have eight jointless green fingers.

The Sun is at the centre of our solar system.
It is the largest star in our solar system and like other stars it generates its heat through nuclear fusion in its core. The heat and light that comes from the Sun is essential for life on Earth. It provides energy for plants to grow, which animal life needs to eat to live.

CORE
15,000,000°C

RADIOACTIVE ZONE
The energy generated from the core takes 170,000 years to travel through this area.

PHOTOSPHERE
5,505°C
The photosphere is the surface of the Sun, although there are two further layers of gas that are above it: the chromosphere and the corona.

SUNSPOTS
These are cooler spots on the Sun, which is why they appear darker.

SOLAR FLARES
These are explosions on the surface of the Sun that occur when a big build up of energy is released.

170,000 YEARS

Most of the visible light from the Sun comes from the fact that it is hot.

HOW CLOSE CAN WE GET?

The better your protective clothing or equipment, the closer you can get towards the Sun without being harmed. Some scientists believe that a spacecraft could get as close as **2,092,147 km** to the Sun. In a specially designed spacesuit an astronaut could get as close as **4,828,032 km**, but would not survive for long before dying from the heat.

The Sun's heat reduces the further you travel to the outer limits of our solar system.

4,828,032 km

4,828,031 km

2,092,146 km

2,092,147 km

1,000,000 KM
2,000,000 KM
3,000,000 KM
4,000,000 KM
5,000,000 KM

DO NOT LOOK DIRECTLY INTO THE SUN!

Looking directly into the Sun will damage your eyesight and could cause permanent blindness. Do not even look into the Sun when wearing sunglasses, as these do not offer sufficient protection. You should use specially designed solar binoculars or eclipse glasses that are fitted with special solar filters.

The temperature at the core of the Earth is **5430°C**, not too far off the temperature on the surface of the Sun.

The average temperature of the Earth's surface is **14°C**.

The hottest place on the Earth are the deserts near the equator, reaching up to **57.7°C**.

The coldest place on the Earth is around the South Pole at **-89°C**.

500°C

400°C

100°C

0°C

-100°C

-200°C

Venus

Mercury

Earth

Mars

Jupiter

Saturn

Uranus

Neptune

Galileo Galilei died under house arrest because of his revolutionary scientific discoveries about space. Here are a few other astronomers who have studied the stars...

ARISTOTLE 384 BCE-322 BCE

Aristotle proved that the Earth was spherical. He pointed out that during a lunar eclipse the shadow of the Earth across the Moon was always circular, proving the Earth to be round. An eclipse is when an object hides our view of another object. In a lunar eclipse this is the Earth's shadow limiting what we can see of the Moon.

Aristotle also pointed out that as you travelled further north or south, the positions of the stars in the sky change. There are constellations visible in the north that you cannot see in the south and vice versa.

The belief that all planets in our solar system orbit the Sun is called heliocentric. This is the model of the Universe that Galilei supported.

The belief that the Earth is at the centre of our solar sytem, around which the Sun and planets orbit, is called geocentric.

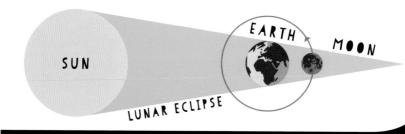

SUN   EARTH   MOON

LUNAR ECLIPSE

JOHANNES KEPLER 1571-1630

It had been thought that the planets followed a perfectly circular orbit around the Sun, but Kepler discovered that their orbital paths are actually elliptical.

SUN

ISAAC NEWTON 1643-1727

Newton suggested that the force that keeps things in place and pulls things together is gravity. This is why apples fall to the ground and why the Earth orbits the Sun.

Newton proved that the force of gravity is stronger the greater the mass of the object, which is one of the reasons why the Moon orbits the Earth and not the other way round. Before Newton proved this, it was believed that the planets were held in place by an invisible shield. He also devised a mathematical model that accurately predicts the movements of planetary objects.

CLAUDIUS PTOLEMY 90-168

Ptolemy accepted the geocentric model of the Solar System, but believed that the planets revolved around a further circle than that of their main orbit. He also established the order of the Solar System that was almost correct.

| Earth | Moon | Mercury | Venus | Sun | Mars | Jupiter | Saturn |

NICOLAUS COPERNICUS 1473-1543

In 1542, Copernicus published a book called *On the Revolutions of the Celestial Spheres* arguing that the Sun, not the Earth, is at the centre of the Universe. This established the heliocentric universe (*helios* being the Greek word for Sun).

GALILEO GALILEI 1564-1642

Galilei built one of the first telescopes and made many astronomical discoveries, including the large moons of Jupiter, sunspots on the Sun, and mountains and valleys on the surface of the Moon.

Galilei supported Copernicus's belief in a heliocentric universe. However, whereas Copernicus only received mild objections to his system, the Catholic Church imprisoned Galilei for supporting it. He died while under house arrest.

ALBERT EINSTEIN 1879-1955

Einstein viewed the Universe as held within space-time. Space-time is like a stretched rubber sheet which is warped by large objects positioned upon it, like the Sun and the planets. These objects cause space-time to bend. This bend is felt as gravity. Einstein proved that light bends in the presence of a large gravitational field, such as around this bend within space-time. He also proved that time goes more slowly in areas with low gravity, where there is less of a bend.

75-76 YEARS FOR AN APPEARANCE OF HALLEY'S COMET

Comets are balls of ice, rock and dust that go around the Sun in a highly elliptical orbit. They go to the outer reaches of our solar system and can take anything from **three** to **1,000 years** to complete their orbit.

ORBIT

SUN

HALLEY'S COMET IS NAMED AFTER EDMOND HALLEY

Edmond Halley was the first person to demonstrate the periodic return of a comet. He proposed that a comet sighted in 1531 was the same comet that had appeared in 1607 and again in 1682. He predicted that this comet would return in 1759. His prediction was correct.

1531   1607   1682   1759

In fact the appearance of Halley's Comet has been traced much further back through history, with one possible sighting recorded in a Chinese chronicle dating from 240 BCE. It is also recorded on the Bayeaux Tapestry from 1066.

BAD OMENS

Comets have at times been considered as bad omens, warning of terrible times ahead.

COMET SEEN IN 1347
Outbreak of the Black Death around the world, killing over **25,000,000** people.

COMET SEEN IN 1066
King Harold II died at the Battle of Hastings with the Norman-French gaining the rule of England. This is the comet that appears on the Bayeaux Tapestry.

HALLEY'S COMET
can be seen from Earth for roughly **five months**, although this depends on local pollution levels. For a large portion of this time it will be only visible from the Southern Hemisphere. It will also spend a lot of this time very near to the Sun, so that viewing it with the naked eye will be near impossible.

COMET SEEN IN 79 CE
The eruption of the volcano Vesuvius that wiped out the city of Pompeii in Italy.

COMET SEEN IN 70 CE
The Siege of Jerusalem, where the Roman army invaded causing mass destruction to the city.

Halley's Comet returns every **75-76 years**. It will next be visible in our sky in 2061.

SOUTHERN HEMISPHERE

Comets are sometimes referred to as 'dirty snowballs'. The amount of dirt, rock and gravel compacted by ice make it look like the kind of snowball you don't want thrown at you.

ANATOMY OF A COMET

A comet speeds up the nearer it gets to the Sun. The combination of increased sunlight and speed causes parts of the comet to fragment, creating **two tails**: a dust tail and a gas tail. The tails can stretch out for **millions of kilometres**.

As a comet gets nearer to the Sun it develops an atmosphere around it, which is called a coma. The coma can grow to become **thousands of kilometres** in diameter.

A main part of a comet is the nucleus which is the compacted rock, dust and ice. The nucleus may only be a **few kilometres** wide.

Like the Moon, a comet is made visible by reflecting the light from the Sun.

Some scientists believe that comets brought water to Earth, allowing life to begin.

GAS TAIL

DUST TAIL

COMA

Comets are roughly the size of a small town.

NUCLEUS

What are moons?

Moons are planetary objects that orbit planets. Moons are always smaller in size to the planets they orbit and can be made of similar rocks and gases.

How are moons formed?

There are three different theories as to how moons are formed.

1. Moons are pieces of their planets that have fallen away.

2. Moons are debris created from the impact of two planets colliding.

3. Moons are wandering elements formed from somewhere else in the Solar System.

As astronomers are able to see more clearly into space, more moons are discovered. Uranus' **27 moons** have been spotted over a period of **216 years**.

1787	1851	1948	1985	1986	1997	1999	2001	2003
))	))	)	)	))))))))))	))	)))	)))	)))

WHILE PLANETS ORBIT THE SUN, MOONS ORBIT THE PLANETS.

Planets	Number of moons
Mercury	
Venus	
Earth	)
Mars	))
Jupiter	))))))))))))))))))))))))))))))))))))))))))))))))
Saturn	))))))))))))))))))))))))))))))))))))))))))))))))))))))))))
Uranus	)))))))))))))))))))))))))))
Neptune	)))))))))))))

MOONS ARE ALSO KNOWN AS 'NATURAL SATELLITES'

and are not to be confused with the mechanical satellites that are put into space to transmit communication back to Earth.

180

8,000

There are approximately **180** natural satellites in our solar system and **8,000** communication satellites.

OUR MOON

The Moon does not produce light of its own but reflects the light from the Sun.

The Sun only lights up the half of the Moon that faces towards it.

The side of the Moon that we never see is called the far or dark side of the Moon.

As the Moon moves around Earth, we see different parts of the half that is lit by the Sun. The different shapes that we see are called phases. There are **eight phases**, all with different names.

FIRST QUARTER

WAXING CRESCENT

WAXING GIBBOUS

NEW

FULL

WANING GIBBOUS

WANING CRESCENT

THIRD QUARTER

27.3 DAYS
The Moon orbits the Earth once every **27.3 days.** The Moon orbits the Earth in an anti-clockwise direction.

Northern Hemisphere

Southern Hemisphere

The Moon also takes **27.3 days** to spin around once on its axis, which means that the same side of the Moon always faces Earth. However, in the Southern Hemisphere the Moon is seen upside down to the view seen in the Northern Hemisphere.

25

24 HOURS FOR EARTH TO ROTATE

Earth moves in two ways: it travels in orbit around the Sun and it rotates on its axis. It takes 24 hours to rotate on its axis.

Axis

An axis is an imaginary line around which an object spins. The Earth's axis is from the North Pole to the South Pole.

Axis

Earth rotates in an anti-clockwise direction.

Anti-clockwise

Earth is tilted at a **23.5 degree angle**.

23.5°

Sun never sets

Equator

Northern Hemisphere

Long days

Southern Hemisphere

Equal days and nights

Short days

The part facing towards the Sun is in daylight while the part facing away from the Sun is in darkness. This means that when the Northern Hemisphere is tilted towards the Sun, places in this hemisphere get more than **12 hours** of daylight, while places in the Southern Hemisphere are tilted away from the Sun and get less than **12 hours** daylight. On the Equator there are always **12 hours** of daylight.

EAST

WEST

THE SUN RISES TOWARDS THE EAST AND SETS TOWARDS THE WEST.
During the day it appears to follow a curved path across the sky. This apparent movement is not caused by the movement of the Sun, but by the Earth spinning on its axis.

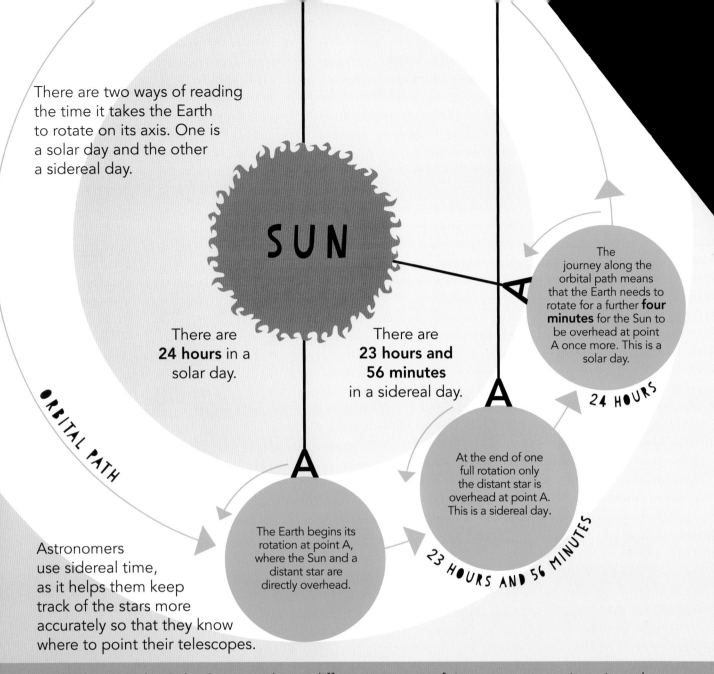

There are two ways of reading the time it takes the Earth to rotate on its axis. One is a solar day and the other a sidereal day.

SUN

There are **24 hours** in a solar day.

There are **23 hours and 56 minutes** in a sidereal day.

The journey along the orbital path means that the Earth needs to rotate for a further **four minutes** for the Sun to be overhead at point A once more. This is a solar day.

ORBITAL PATH

The Earth begins its rotation at point A, where the Sun and a distant star are directly overhead.

At the end of one full rotation only the distant star is overhead at point A. This is a sidereal day.

24 HOURS

23 HOURS AND 56 MINUTES

Astronomers use sidereal time, as it helps them keep track of the stars more accurately so that they know where to point their telescopes.

Each planet in the Solar System takes a different amount of time to rotate on its axis and therefore the lengths of their days are all different.

HOURS IN A DAY (SIDEREAL TIME)

5,832
1,465
26
22
18
14
10
6
2

MERCURY VENUS EARTH MARS JUPITER SATURN URANUS NEPTUNE

EAR FOR THE EARTH TO ORBIT THE SUN

...ys

the Earth takes one year ...t actually takes **365.25** days.

The **.25 day** (quarter of a day) means that every **four years** there is an extra day and so rather than **365 days**, that year has **366 days**. It is known as a leap year and falls on **29 February**.

There is a **1** in **1,461** chance of being born on

29 FEBRUARY.

People born on a leapday are called **leaplings**.

Leaplings have to wait four years before they can 'officially' celebrate their birthdays.

I AM 3

I AM 15

Born 29 February

Born 28 February

In some countries it was a tradition that women could only propose to men on a leap day.

ORBITING SPEEDS The Milky Way, the Solar System and the Earth all travel at different speeds.

1,080,000 km/h

828,000 km/h

108,000 km/h

Speed of a cheetah
112.65 km/h

EARTH TRAVELS 940 MILLION KM DURING ONE ORBIT

To travel the same distance that the Earth covers in one orbit, you would have to walk the distance between Scotland and Australia **64,661 times**, or New York, USA, to Australia **56,674 times**.

x 64,661

x 55,674

The Earth's orbit around the Sun is elliptical and so the distance between the Earth and Sun varies throughout the year.

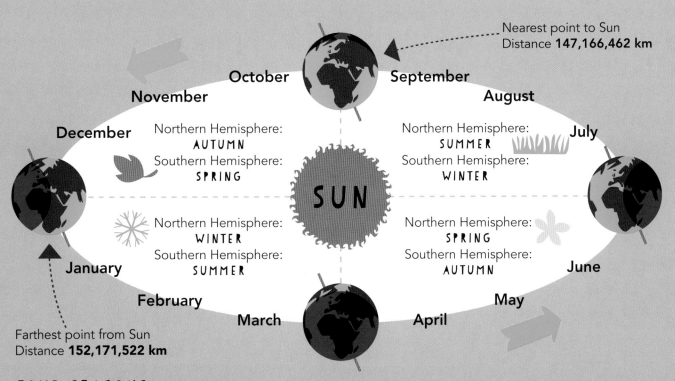

Nearest point to Sun
Distance **147,166,462 km**

October September

November August

December July

Northern Hemisphere:
AUTUMN
Southern Hemisphere:
SPRING

Northern Hemisphere:
SUMMER
Southern Hemisphere:
WINTER

SUN

Northern Hemisphere:
WINTER
Southern Hemisphere:
SUMMER

Northern Hemisphere:
SPRING
Southern Hemisphere:
AUTUMN

January June

February May

March April

Farthest point from Sun
Distance **152,171,522 km**

FOUR SEASONS

The change in temperature and sunlight that each season experiences is caused by the tilt on the Earth's axis as it rotates and travels along its orbit around the Sun.

When the Northern Hemisphere is tilted away from the Sun, it is winter in this hemisphere and summer in the Southern Hemisphere. So while the Northern Hemisphere is having summer, autumn, winter and spring, the Southern Hemisphere is having the opposite: winter, spring, summer and autumn.

FURTHER INFORMATION

BOOKS

Know It All: Space by Andrew Langley (Franklin Watts, 2013)
The Real Scientist: Space! by Peter Riley (Franklin Watts, 2012)
Science F.A.Q.: Why Are Black Holes Black? by Thomas Canavan
(Franklin Watts 2013)
The World of Infographics: Space by Jon Richards and Ed Simkins
(Wayland, 2012)

WEBSITES

BBC Newsround's website containing great videos, news, facts and
quizzes:
www.bbc.co.uk/newsround/14082427
NASA's website for kids, containing games, videos and pictures:
www.nasa.gov/audience/forkids/kidsclub/flash/index.html
Quizzes and fact files on space:
www.sciencekids.co.nz/space.html

Note to parents and teachers:
Every effort has been made by the publisher to ensure that these websites contain no
inappropriate or offensive material. However, because of the nature of the Internet, it is
impossible to guarantee that the content of these sites will not be altered. We strongly
advise that Internet access is supervised by a responsible adult.

LARGE NUMBERS

1,000,000,000,000,000,000,000,000,000,000,000 = ONE DECILLION

1,000,000,000,000,000,000,000,000,000,000 = ONE NONILLION

1,000,000,000,000,000,000,000,000,000 = ONE OCTILLION

1,000,000,000,000,000,000,000,000 = ONE SEPTILLION

1,000,000,000,000,000,000,000 = ONE SEXTILLION

1,000,000,000,000,000,000 = ONE QUINTILLION

1,000,000,000,000,000 = ONE QUADRILLION

1,000,000,000,000 = ONE TRILLION

1,000,000,000 = ONE BILLION

1,000,000 = ONE MILLION

1000 = ONE THOUSAND

100 = ONE HUNDRED

10 = TEN

1 = ONE

GLOSSARY

alien	a creature from another world
asteroid	rocks, smaller than planets, that orbit the Sun
astronaut	a person trained to go into space
astronomer	person who studies the stars
axis	an imaginary line around which a planet rotates
Big Bang	an explosion that marked the birth of the Universe
black hole	an area in space that has a strong gravitational force at its centre
cluster	a group of similar objects
comet	object made of ice and dust orbiting around the Sun
constellation	a group of stars
eclipse	the view of an object hidden by another
elliptical	relating to an oval shape
equator	an imaginary line drawn around the Earth separating the Northern and Southern Hemispheres
estimate	an approximate calculation
galaxy	a collection of planets and stars held together by gravity
geocentric	belief that the Earth is at the centre of the Solar System
gravity	a force that pulls objects together
heliocentric	belief that the Sun is at the centre of the Solar System
humanoid	resembling a human
leapling	a person born on 29 February, a leap day
meteor	piece of space rock smaller than an asteroid
meteorite	the name for a meteor that has landed on Earth
nuclear fusion	a process where two elements combine to create another element, releasing large amounts of energy
observatory	a building designed to help see into space using telescopes
omen	an occurrence that suggests bad things to come
orbit	a curved path an object follows going around another object
phases	stages of development
phenomena	unusual occurrences
planetary	relating to planets
prediction	a thing told about the future
psychological	relating to the mind and mental activity
radioactive	emissions in response to a nuclear reaction
satellite	an object placed in orbit around a planet
sidereal day	time it takes the Earth to make a full rotation in alignment to a distant star
solar day	time it takes the Earth to make a rotation in alignment with the Sun
star	a bright shining ball of gas in the night sky
telescope	an instrument designed to make distant objects appear near
UFO	stands for Unidentified Flying Object, an unexplained object in the sky

INDEX